SO-AYZ-598

stepping off the beaten path

IN PURSUIT OF JESUS

RICK AND BEV LAWRENCE

Group

LOVELAND, COLORADO
www.group.com

In Pursuit of Jesus
Copyright © 2008 Rick and Bev Lawrence

Visit our website: **group.com**

Credits
Editor: Brad Lewis
Developer: Roxanne Wieman
Project Manager: Scott M. Kinner
Chief Creative Officer: Joani Schultz
Copy Editor: Dena Twinem
Art Director: Jeff Storm
Print Production Artist: The DesignWorks Group, Inc.
Cover Art Director/Designer: Jeff Storm
Production Manager: DeAnne Lear

ISBN: 978-0-7644-3678-9

10 9 8 7 6 5 4   17 16 15 14 13

IN PURSUIT OF JESUS

ACKNOWLEDGMENTS

First, we'd like to thank Jesus, who romanced us into pursuing him in the first place—we (only) love because he loved us first.

Second, we'd like to thank all the people who took a chance and gave in to their curiosity and thirst to show up to a study that was way out of the box for many. We treasure your tears, your laughter, your life-changing insights, and the sense of "family" you brought to this pursuit.

Third, we'd like to thank our daughters, Lucy and Emma, who got up early on Sunday, for so many Sundays, so we could teach this study. For Lucy, who ended up actually participating in the class and adding profound insights—we loved your presence with us. For Emma, who had to hear Dad say, "Not right now, honey" about a thousand times while I finished preparing this study for publication—we appreciate your patience with us.

Fourth, we'd like to thank the leaders in our church—particularly Bob Krulish, Anthony Vartuli, and Tom Melton—who believe in Jesus, us, and this study.

DEDICATION

To our dear daughters Lucy and Emma.
Our prayers over you have always been that you would have
hearts that burn for Jesus—as you grow,
we hope he's more and more your consuming passion.
We love you, dears.

IN PURSUIT OF JESUS

CONTENTS

IN PURSUIT OF JESUS

INTRODUCTION

We birthed this 10-week adventure into the heart of Jesus out of passion and desperation. At the time, we had no thoughts of anyone other than us leading people on this pursuit. After years of going to church classes and small groups that tried to focus on Jesus and the great truths of Scripture, we felt unsatisfied with our experiences. In those learning environments, we often felt like we'd been invited to a feast at a friend's house, but when we showed up, we found crackers and cheese as the main course. Sure, we ate something, but it was no feast.

We were hungry for more. More of Jesus.

In fact, we *had to* have more of Jesus. We needed him like two thirsty survivors crawling toward a well in the desert. So we decided to create the kind of study we wished we could go to. We came up with 10 "snapshots" of Jesus that seemed worth pursuing. Then we plunged ourselves into each one with a determination not just to get at the truth of Jesus, but to do so in an engaging, experiential, and interactive way that also honored what participants in the class would bring to the table.

We set before ourselves and the "family" gathered around this class the overarching question that Jesus asked his disciples after the feeding of the 5,000 (Luke 9:12-20): "Who do you say I am?" Our simple mission: Spend 10 weeks exploring our answer to that question. Further, we wanted to go beyond answering that question only with our heads; we very much wanted to respond to the question with our hearts.

You can understand the truth about Jesus in a lot of different ways—just as you can understand the truth about your spouse or best friend in different ways. Not all of these ways have to do with hard facts; many have to do more with your "heart knowledge" of the person. The reason you marry someone or hang out with someone has as much to do with your emotional experience as your "factual" assessment of who someone is.

After the pursuit was over and we had a chance to catch our breath, we realized we'd been a part of something powerful. When we saw people who'd attended the class in the hallways at church—a wide spectrum of participants from teenagers to senior adults—they stopped us with a kind of a hunger in their eyes to ask when we planned to offer the class again. Many expressed that for the first time, their insights and input were passionately valued in the study. We not only gave participants the opportunity to think more critically and make their own discoveries about Jesus, we kind of forced them to do it. And they loved it because they "owned" it! They loved the atmosphere of participation, dignity, and respect that grew up around our joint pursuit.

Bev and I believe that true transformation comes when you get closer to Jesus. We feel so strongly about this, I'm tempted to just write that sentence again:

We believe that true transformation comes when you get closer to Jesus.

The aim of this pursuit isn't just to get closer to Jesus, but to get infected by him. To move him from the fringes of everyday life to the bull's-eye of everyday life.

As you prepare to launch into this adventure, know that we're with you. We couldn't be more excited about the journey you're about to take!

—RICK AND BEV LAWRENCE

IN PURSUIT OF JESUS

A LESSON ABOUT LEARNING

This study probably differs from most studies you've been a part of. Instead of listening to what amounts to a lecture or filling in blanks in a book, your leader will invite you to be a full participant in the learning. That means you'll take part in a lot of conversations and times of feedback. And you'll dig deep for truths about Jesus from music, film, art, and experiences. Your main responsibility will be to play. We mean, as you embark on this adventure with others, keep in mind that everyone's insights and perspectives are crucial. So we urge you to play along with these adventures. Join in and jump in to new experiences and a new way of learning about Jesus. By the end of these 10 weeks, you'll find yourself closer to Jesus—likely much closer to Jesus. And when you get close to Jesus, who knows what could happen?

So, each time you join this pursuit, you need just five things:

1. This booklet
2. A pen
3. A Bible
4. Eager curiosity
5. That ability to "play" with new experiences.

As kids, we all possess a healthy curiosity. But as we grow older, we gain some life experience and start thinking we have things figured out pretty well. But we know from experience that all of us can grow more curious as we get older. In fact, because we're more experienced and more mature people, all of us have a growing capacity for curiosity.

So don't hold back in this study. Dive in! If you do, you'll encounter Jesus as he really is—and no one has ever been more beautiful than Jesus.

IN PURSUIT OF JESUS

WEEK 1: WHO DO YOU SAY I AM?

RON BURGUNDY INTERVIEWS JESUS

▶ What did you see in this interview that shows what people seem to think about Jesus?

THOMAS AND PHILIP AND JESUS

" 'You know the way to the place where I am going.' Thomas said to him, 'Lord, we don't know where you are going, so how can we know the way?' Jesus answered, 'I am the way and the truth and the life. No one comes to the Father except through me. If you really knew me, you would know my Father as well. From now on, you do know him and have seen him.' Philip said, 'Lord, show us the Father and that will be enough for us.' Jesus answered: 'Don't you know me, Philip, even after I have been among you such a long time? Anyone who has seen me has seen the Father' " (John 14:4-9).

▶ Are the disciples stupid or thick or slow or…what? Why do they have such a hard time understanding Jesus?

THE 95/45/10 PROBLEM

▶ For the 95 percent-ers—or even the 45 percent-ers—why isn't Jesus the central focus of their lives? What accounts for this 95-45-10 progression in our culture?

JOHN ELDREDGE

"I am convinced beyond a doubt of this: God wants to be loved. He wants to be a priority to someone. How could we have missed this? From cover to cover, from beginning to end, the cry of God's heart is, 'Why won't you choose me?' It is amazing to me how humble, how *vulnerable* God is on this point. 'You will…find me,' says the Lord, 'when you seek me with all your heart' (Jer. 29:13). In other words, 'Look for me, pursue me—I want you to pursue me.' Amazing. As Tozer says, 'God waits to be wanted.' " [1]

MIMI WILSON (BIBLE TEACHER, SPEAKER, AUTHOR)

"We'll be shaped by who we think God is—that's why God told us not to worship idols."

HOW DO YOU SEE JESUS?

In the space below, write some words that describe the way you see Jesus. Don't write canned phrases from the Bible or other words you think you should write. Instead, be brutally honest with yourself. How do you *really* experience Jesus, and what do you *really* think of him?

DISCUSS IN PAIRS

Think about your list of descriptive words. Think about one way you've been shaped by the way you see Jesus. Share with your partner.

TOM MELTON

"We don't *really* believe Jesus is beautiful, because we wouldn't describe our relationship with him as so much work if we did." [2]

PURSUING GOD

"One thing I ask of the Lord, this is what I seek: that I may dwell in the house of the Lord all the days of my life, to gaze upon the beauty of the Lord and to seek him in his temple" (Psalm 27:4).

DISTANCE LIST

Write as many descriptive words as you can about your partner at the other end of the room.

SIX-INCH LIST

Write descriptive words about your partner that you missed before.

DEBRIEF

Look at your lists, and answer:

▶ What changed in your descriptive words when you got closer?

▶ What's something you liked and didn't like about getting closer?

▶ How might getting closer to Jesus change your perspective of him?

▶ What's good about getting closer to Jesus, and what's hard about getting closer to him?

THE PROGRESSION

Get to know Jesus well, because the more you know him, the more you'll love him, and the more you love him, the more you'll want to follow him, and the more you follow him, the more you'll become like him, and the more you become like him, the more you become yourself.

▶ What do you think that last line means: The more you become like him, the more become yourself?

THE BIG QUESTION

Luke 9:12-20

JOHN ELDREDGE

"God yearns to be known. But he wants to be *sought after* by those who would know him. He says, 'You will seek me and find me when you seek me with all your heart' (Jer. 29:13). There is dignity here; God does not throw himself at any passerby. He is no harlot. If you would know him you must love him; you must seek him with your whole heart." [3]

ENDNOTE 1: John Eldredge, *Wild at Heart* (Thomas Nelson Publishers, 2001), p. 36.
ENDNOTE 2: From an unpublished sermon by Tom Melton, pastor of Greenwood Community Church in Denver.
ENDNOTE 3: John and Stasi Eldredge, *Captivating: Unveiling the Mystery of a Woman's Soul* (Thomas Nelson Publishers, 2005), p. 41.

IN PURSUIT OF JESUS

WEEK 2: JESUS DEFINES "GOOD"

TASTE AND SEE

▶ What makes a treat taste so good?

▶ Do people generally agree on what tastes good and what doesn't?

▶ How do we know when something tastes good to us and when it doesn't?

NOTHING BUT JESUS

"And when I came to you, brethren, I did not come with superiority of speech or of wisdom, proclaiming to you the testimony of God. For I determined to know nothing among you except Jesus Christ, and Him crucified" (1 Corinthians 2:1-2, NAS).

HIDE-AND-SEEK JESUS

▶ What misconceptions about Jesus does this little clip poke fun at?

DEFINING "GOOD"

Take two minutes right now to list as many things as you can think of that are "good." Think about what you'd classify as fundamentally good. Your list can include anything. It doesn't have to be "spiritual."

▶ Share your list with a partner, then talk about how you decide what's good and what's not. What's your criteria for "good"?

JESUS DEFINES "GOOD"

"A certain ruler asked him, 'Good teacher, what must I do to inherit eternal life?' 'Why do you call me good?' Jesus answered. 'No one is good—except God alone. You know the commandments: "Do not commit adultery, do not murder, do not steal, do not give false testimony, honor your father and mother." ' 'All these I have kept since I was a boy,' he said. When Jesus heard this, he said to him, 'You still lack one thing. Sell everything you have and give to the poor, and you will have treasure in heaven. Then come, follow me.' When he heard this, he became very sad, because he was a man of great wealth" (Luke 18:18-23).

▶ Why did Jesus respond the way he did with this young man?

▶ Why did Jesus tell him to sell everything he had and follow him?

"I AM THE VINE"

Jesus says, "I am the vine; you are the branches" (John 15:5). Our life, our goodness, is ultimately tied to Jesus. We can try to make it on our own, imagining that we're a "vine" when we're really a "branch." But in reality, without him, we have no life, no goodness. According to Jesus, only he is good.

OUR GUIDE

"Taste and see that the Lord is good" (Psalm 34:8).

TASTE TEST

Your mission is to list every single taste you can discern. For example, if you wanted to make this yourself without a recipe, what would you include?

Use "A Taste Test" on page 23 to record your answers. Answer the questions for one steak sauce first, and then the other. The leader will tell you when to switch to the other sauce.

▶ What connections can we make from improving our palate to improving our ability to taste Jesus well?

TASTE-TEST CHALLENGE

With your partner, read the passage assigned by your leader. Then discuss:

What did Jesus do that was good? List as many things as you can.

- ▶ Luke 4:1-13: Jesus tempted by the devil

- ▶ Luke 5:27-32: Jesus calls Matthew (called Levi before he became a disciple), parties with tax collectors

- ▶ Luke 6:6-11: Jesus heals man's withered hand on Sabbath

- ▶ Luke 8:26-39: Jesus casts demons out of Gerasene demoniac

- ▶ Luke 12:1-12: Jesus gives warnings and encouragements

- ▶ Luke 14:16-24: Parable of the dinner

- ▶ Why do these words and actions represent "good"?

- ▶ What's surprising about the "goodness" of Jesus' words and actions?

- ▶ What can you pick out about what Jesus likes and doesn't like from these stories?

CLOSING RESPONSE

Think about how God is bigger to you than when you walked into this room. In the quiet, think of the words that remind you of how you tasted God today—write them here if you'd like.

A TASTE TEST

Steak Sauce 1

List every single taste you can discern—
for example, if you were going to make
this yourself without a recipe, what would
you include? Your sense of smell can help
you here.

Steak Sauce 2

List every single taste you can discern—
for example, if you were going to make
this yourself without a recipe, what would
you include? Your sense of smell can help
you here.

WEEK 3: JESUS AND HIS PARABLES

PARABLE THROUGH SONG

Close your eyes and listen to the song "Grace" by U2. If you want to refer to the song summary, turn to page 29.

YOUR STORIES

Take a few minutes to ask God to bring to mind *a story*—a specific story—that describes what it was like to grow up in your home as a child. Write a short version (just a few words or sentences) below.

Now take a few minutes to ask God to bring to mind *a story*—a specific story—that captures the essence of either your father or mother. Write a short version (just a few words or sentences) below.

"Taste" your partner's story by slowing down and focusing well. Pay attention. Look for gaps or unexplained statements in the story. Ask questions that get at the impact of your partner's story.

JESUS' PARABLES

Jesus told 55 parables—they make up a large percentage of his "teaching." If you collect all the parables together, almost all of them answer one (or both) of these questions:

▶ Who is God?

▶ What is life like in God's kingdom (his home)?

THE WAYS OF GOD

"For my thoughts are not your thoughts, neither are your ways my ways" (Isaiah 55:8).

▶ What are "the ways" of God?

CUSTOMS AND TRADITIONS

"The disciples came to him and asked, 'Why do you speak to the people in parables?' He replied, 'The knowledge of the secrets of the kingdom of heaven has been given to you, but not to them. Whoever has will be given more, and he will have an abundance. Whoever does not have, even what he has will be taken from him. This is why I speak to them in parables: Though seeing, they do not see; though hearing, they do not hear or understand' " (Matthew 13:10-13).

▶ What did Jesus mean by this explanation of why he spoke in parables?

THE KINGDOM OF GOD IS LIKE...

As a trio, read the parable assigned by your leader and list as many truths you can about the values, practices, and priorities of the kingdom of God. (See page 30 for the text of the parables.)

▶ Parable of Wheat and Weeds—Matthew 13:24-30

▶ Parable of the Pine Nut—Matthew 13:31-32

▶ Parable of the Yeast—Matthew 13:33

▶ Parable of the Treasure in the Field—Matthew 13:44

▶ Parable of the Pearl of Great Price—Matthew 13:45-46

▶ Parable of the Big Fishnet—Matthew 13:47-50

UNDERSTANDING GOD'S PRIORITIES

"He said to them, 'Therefore every teacher of the law who has been instructed about the kingdom of heaven is like the owner of a house who brings out of his storeroom new treasures as well as old' " (Matthew 13:52).

▶ What happens when you understand and follow the ways of Jesus' family?

THE CHARACTER OF GOD IS LIKE...

As a trio, read aloud the parable assigned by your leader and list as many truths you can about the nature, personality, values, priorities, and passions of the person of God. (See page 32 for the text of the parables.)

▶ Parable of the Great Physician—Matthew 9:10-13

▶ Parable of the Moneylender—Luke 7:40-47

▶ Parable of the Lost Sheep—Luke 15:3-7

▶ Parable of the Lost Coin—Luke 15:8-10

▶ Parable of the Prodigal Son—Luke 15:11-32

THE PARABLES CONTINUE

Quietly, take a few minutes to ask God to bring to mind an event that happened to you in the last week. This might be anything that sticks out to you. Write a short description of the event or happening. Don't think too hard about this. Just write down a few words or sentences about the first thing that comes to your mind.

Now take a few minutes to ask God how this event or happening might be a parable in your life. How is God's voice or message to you locked up in the story?

How does your little parable-story answer one of these two questions:

▶ Who is God?

▶ What is life like in God's kingdom?

Don't "create" the meaning behind the story. Instead, simply ask God to show you the meaning. Wait quietly until you sense the meaning coming to the surface of your mind, and then write the meaning here.

CLOSING

If you desire, use the space below to reflect on the closing song, "Step by Step" by Rich Mullins.

"GRACE" BY U2

(Song Summary)

This song is about grace—it could be a name or it could be an idea.

Grace "takes the blame" and "covers the shame" and "removes the stain."

Grace is both a girl's name and an act of God that rescued us all.

Grace is beautiful—the most beautiful thing—because grace can take what's ugly and make it beautiful.

Grace knows how to act in every situation—and grace knows how to patiently pursue us.

Grace has nothing to do with the "you get what you deserve" system of the world.

When you're experiencing grace, you can sense God's beauty—because God's grace "finds beauty in everything."

Grace is a working mother—the grace of God is at work in the down-and-dirty of our lives. Her hands are those of a hard worker, not a privileged queen.

Grace points, always, to the pearl of great price, who is Jesus himself. Jesus takes away the "stain" of our sin through grace.

Because we've all been made beautiful by God's grace—he's taken the "ugly" we've offered him (all we have) and made it good.

KINGDOM OF GOD PARABLES

THE PARABLE OF WHEAT AND WEEDS

Matthew 13:24-30 (The Message)

He told another story. "God's kingdom is like a farmer who planted good seed in his field. That night, while his hired men were asleep, his enemy sowed thistles all through the wheat and slipped away before dawn. When the first green shoots appeared and the grain began to form, the thistles showed up, too.

"The farmhands came to the farmer and said, 'Master, that was clean seed you planted, wasn't it? Where did these thistles come from?' He answered, 'Some enemy did this.' The farmhands asked, 'Should we weed out the thistles?'

"He said, 'No, if you weed the thistles, you'll pull up the wheat, too. Let them grow together until harvest time. Then I'll instruct the harvesters to pull up the thistles and tie them in bundles for the fire, then gather the wheat and put it in the barn.' "

THE PARABLE OF THE PINE NUT

Matthew 13:31-32 (The Message)

Another story. "God's kingdom is like a pine nut that a farmer plants. It is quite small as seeds go, but in the course of years it grows into a huge pine tree, and eagles build nests in it."

THE PARABLE OF THE YEAST

Matthew 13:33 (The Message)

Another story. "God's kingdom is like yeast that a woman works into the dough for dozens of loaves of barley bread—and waits while the dough rises."

THE PARABLE OF THE TREASURE IN THE FIELD
Matthew 13:44 (The Message)

"God's kingdom is like a treasure hidden in a field for years and then accidentally found by a trespasser. The finder is ecstatic—what a find!—and proceeds to sell everything he owns to raise money and buy that field."

THE PARABLE OF THE PEARL OF GREAT PRICE
Matthew 13:45-46 (The Message)

"Or, God's kingdom is like a jewel merchant on the hunt for excellent pearls. Finding one that is flawless, he immediately sells everything and buys it."

THE PARABLE OF THE BIG FISHNET
Matthew 13:47-50 (The Message)

"Or, God's kingdom is like a fishnet cast into the sea, catching all kinds of fish. When it is full, it is hauled onto the beach. The good fish are picked out and put in a tub; those unfit to eat are thrown away. That's how it will be when the curtain comes down on history. The angels will come and cull the bad fish and throw them in the garbage. There will be a lot of desperate complaining, but it won't do any good."

CHARACTER OF GOD PARABLES

PARABLE OF THE GREAT PHYSICIAN
Matthew 9:10-13 (The Message)

Later when Jesus was eating supper at Matthew's house with his close followers, a lot of disreputable characters came and joined them. When the Pharisees saw him keeping this kind of company, they had a fit, and lit into Jesus' followers. "What kind of example is this from your Teacher, acting cozy with crooks and riffraff?" Jesus, overhearing, shot back, "Who needs a doctor: the healthy or the sick? Go figure out what this Scripture means: 'I'm after mercy, not religion.' I'm here to invite outsiders, not coddle insiders."

PARABLE OF THE MONEYLENDER
Luke 7:40-47 (The Message)

Jesus said to him, "Simon, I have something to tell you." "Oh? Tell me." "Two men were in debt to a banker. One owed five hundred silver pieces, the other fifty. Neither of them could pay up, and so the banker canceled both debts. Which of the two would be more grateful?" Simon answered, "I suppose the one who was forgiven the most." "That's right," said Jesus. Then turning to the woman, but speaking to Simon, he said, "Do you see this woman? I came to your home; you provided no water for my feet, but she rained tears on my feet and dried them with her hair. You gave me no greeting, but from the time I arrived she hasn't quit kissing my feet. You provided nothing for freshening up, but she has soothed my feet with perfume. Impressive, isn't it? She was forgiven many, many sins, and so she is very, very grateful. If the forgiveness is minimal, the gratitude is minimal."

THE PARABLE OF THE LOST SHEEP
Luke 15:3-7 (The Message)

By this time a lot of men and women of doubtful reputation were hanging around Jesus, listening intently. The Pharisees and religion scholars were not pleased, not at all pleased. They growled, "He takes in sinners and eats meals with them, treating them like old friends." Their grumbling triggered this story.

"Suppose one of you had a hundred sheep and lost one. Wouldn't you leave the ninety-nine in the wilderness and go after the lost one until you found it? When found, you can be sure you would put it across your shoulders, rejoicing, and when you got home call in your friends and neighbors, saying, 'Celebrate with me! I've found my lost sheep!' Count on it—there's more joy in heaven over one sinner's rescued life than over ninety-nine good people in no need of rescue."

THE PARABLE OF THE LOST COIN
Luke 15:8-10 (The Message)

"Or imagine a woman who has ten coins and loses one. Won't she light a lamp and scour the house, looking in every nook and cranny until she finds it? And when she finds it you can be sure she'll call her friends and neighbors: 'Celebrate with me! I found my lost coin!' Count on it—that's the kind of party God's angels throw every time one lost soul turns to God."

THE PARABLE OF THE PRODIGAL SON
Luke 15:11-32 (The Message)

Then he said, "There was once a man who had two sons. The younger said to his father, 'Father, I want right now what's coming to me.' So the father divided the property between them. It wasn't long before the younger son packed his bags and left for a distant country. There, undisciplined and dissipated, he wasted everything he had. After he had gone through all his money, there was a bad famine all through that country and he began to hurt. He signed on with a citizen there who assigned him to his fields to slop the pigs. He was so hungry he would have eaten the corncobs in the pig slop, but no one would give him any. That brought him to his senses. He said, 'All those farmhands working for my father sit down to three meals a day, and here I am starving to death. I'm going back to my father. I'll say to him, Father, I've sinned against God, I've sinned before you; I don't deserve to be called your son. Take me on as a hired hand.' He got right up and went home to his father. When he was still a long way off, his father saw him. His heart pounding, he ran out, embraced him, and kissed him. The son started his speech: 'Father, I've sinned against God, I've sinned before you; I don't deserve to be called your son ever again.' But the father wasn't listening. He was calling to the servants, 'Quick. Bring a clean set of clothes and dress him. Put the family ring on his finger and sandals on his feet. Then get a grain-fed heifer and roast it. We're going to feast! We're going to have a wonderful time! My son is here—given up for dead and now alive! Given up for lost and now found!' And they began to have a wonderful time. All this time his older son was out in the field. When the day's work was done he came in. As he approached the house, he heard the music and dancing. Calling over one of the houseboys, he asked what was going on. He told him, 'Your brother came home. Your father has ordered a feast—barbecued beef!—because he has him home safe and sound.' The older brother stalked off in an angry sulk and refused to join in. His father came out and tried to talk to him, but he wouldn't listen. The son said, 'Look how many years I've stayed here serving you, never giving you one moment of grief, but have you ever thrown a party for me and my friends? Then this son of yours who has thrown away your money on whores shows up and you go all out with a feast!' His father said, 'Son, you don't understand. You're with me all the time, and everything that is mine is yours—but this is a wonderful time, and we had to celebrate. This brother of yours was dead, and he's alive! He was lost, and he's found!' "

IN PURSUIT OF JESUS

WEEK 4: JESUS AND THE DESPERATE PEOPLE

OPENING WORSHIP

Andrew Peterson's "The Silence of God." If you'd like to follow along with the song summary, turn to page 41.

THIRSTY FOR JESUS

"Now on the last day, the great day of the feast, Jesus stood and cried out, saying, 'If anyone is thirsty, let him come to Me and drink' " (John 7:37, NAS).

"As the deer pants for the water brooks, So my soul pants for You, O God. My soul thirsts for God, for the living God" (Psalm 42:1-2a, NAS).

FILM CLIP

Discuss the following questions with your partner:

▶ Can you think of a time in your life you felt something like what George Bailey felt in this scene?

▶ Was the "fruit" of that desperation good or bad in your life? Explain.

THE ROLE OF DESPERATION

"Now the serpent was more crafty than any of the wild animals the Lord God had made. He said to the woman, 'Did God really say, "You must not eat from any tree in the garden"?' The woman said to the serpent, 'We may eat fruit from the trees in the garden, but God did say, "You must not eat fruit from the tree that is in the middle of the garden, and you must not touch it, or you will die." ' 'You will not surely die,' the serpent said to the woman. 'For God knows that when you eat of it your eyes will be opened, and you will be like God, knowing good and evil' " (Genesis 3:1-5).

JESUS AND THE DESPERADOES

▶ The disciples who dropped everything to follow Jesus

▶ The woman who touched the hem of Jesus' garment

▶ The prostitute at the party of Pharisees

▶ Zacchaeus the tax collector

▶ The Canaanite woman

▶ What was different about the Desperadoes, compared to what we know about the Pharisees?

▶ How were these individuals different in what they said and did?

▶ What motivated the Desperadoes that seems different from the Pharisees?

▶ What drew Jesus to these people?

▶ Why did Jesus gravitate to and honor the Desperadoes?

▶ What about Jesus draws him to these people?

INVITING JESUS TO ENTER OUR DESPERATION

"Suffering either gives me to myself or it destroys me" (Oswald Chambers, *My Utmost for His Highest*).

▶ Do you think this statement is true? Why?

▶ What does it mean to "receive ourselves" in our suffering?

CLOSING WORSHIP

Andrew Peterson's "Just as I Am." If you'd like to follow along with the song summary, turn to page 42.

THE DESPERADOES

▶ **The Disciples** (Matthew 4:18-22): "As Jesus was walking beside the Sea of Galilee, he saw two brothers, Simon called Peter and his brother Andrew. They were casting a net into the lake, for they were fishermen. 'Come, follow me,' Jesus said, 'and I will make you fishers of men.' At once they left their nets and followed him. Going on from there, he saw two other brothers, James son of Zebedee and his brother John. They were in a boat with their father Zebedee, preparing their nets. Jesus called them, and immediately they left the boat and their father and followed him."

▶ **The Woman With an Issue of Blood** (Matthew 9:18-22)—"While he was saying this, a ruler came and knelt before him and said, 'My daughter has just died. But come and put your hand on her, and she will live.' Jesus got up and went with him, and so did his disciples. Just then a woman who had been subject to bleeding for twelve years came up behind him and touched the edge of his cloak. She said to herself, 'If I only touch his cloak, I will be healed.' Jesus turned and saw her. 'Take heart, daughter,' he said, 'your faith has healed you.' And the woman was healed from that moment."

▶ **The Sinful Woman at the Pharisee's Party** (Luke 7:36-50)—"Now one of the Pharisees invited Jesus to have dinner with him, so he went to the Pharisee's house and reclined at the table. When a woman who had lived a sinful life in that town learned that Jesus was eating at the Pharisee's house, she brought an alabaster jar of perfume, and as she stood behind him at his feet weeping, she began to wet his feet with her tears. Then she wiped them with her hair, kissed them and poured perfume on them. When the Pharisee who had invited him saw this, he said to himself, 'If this man were a prophet, he would know who is touching him and what kind of woman she is—that she is a sinner.' Jesus answered him, 'Simon, I have something to tell you.' 'Tell me, teacher,' he said. 'Two men owed money to a certain moneylender. One owed him five hundred denarii, and the other fifty. Neither of them had the money to pay him back, so he canceled the debts of both. Now which of them will love him more?' Simon replied, 'I suppose the one who had the bigger debt canceled.' 'You have judged correctly,' Jesus said. Then he turned toward the woman and said to Simon, 'Do you see this woman? I came into your house. You did not give me any water for my feet, but she wet my feet with her tears and wiped them with her hair. You did not give me a kiss, but this woman, from the time I entered, has not stopped kissing my feet. You did not put oil on my head, but she has poured perfume on my feet. Therefore, I tell you, her many sins have been forgiven—for she loved much. But he who has been forgiven little loves little.' Then Jesus said to her, 'Your sins are forgiven.' The other guests began to say among themselves, 'Who is this who even forgives sins?' Jesus said to the woman, 'Your faith has saved you; go in peace.' "

▶ **Zacchaeus the Tax Collector** (Luke 19:1-10)—"Jesus entered Jericho and was passing through. A man was there by the name of Zacchaeus; he was a chief tax collector and was wealthy. He wanted to see who Jesus was, but being a short man he could not, because of the crowd. So he ran ahead and climbed a sycamore-fig tree to see him, since Jesus was coming that way. When Jesus reached the spot, he looked up and said to him, 'Zacchaeus, come down immediately. I must stay at your house today.' So he came down at once and welcomed him gladly. All the people saw this and began to mutter, 'He has gone to be the guest of a "sinner." ' But Zacchaeus stood up and said to the Lord, 'Look, Lord! Here and now I give half of my possessions to the poor, and if I have cheated anybody out of anything, I will pay back four times the amount.' Jesus said to him, 'Today salvation has come to this house, because this man, too, is a son of Abraham. For the Son of Man came to seek and to save what was lost.' "

▶ **The Canaanite Woman** (Matthew 15:21-28)—"Leaving that place, Jesus withdrew to the region of Tyre and Sidon. A Canaanite woman from that vicinity came to him, crying out, 'Lord, Son of David, have mercy on me! My daughter is suffering terribly from demon-possession.' Jesus did not answer a word. So his disciples came to him and urged him, 'Send her away, for she keeps crying out after us.' He answered, 'I was sent only to the lost sheep of Israel.' The woman came and knelt before him. 'Lord, help me!' she said. He replied, 'It is not right to take the children's bread and toss it to their dogs.' 'Yes, Lord,' she said, 'but even the dogs eat the crumbs that fall from their masters' table.' Then Jesus answered, 'Woman, you have great faith! Your request is granted.' And her daughter was healed from that very hour."

RECEIVING YOURSELF IN THE FIRES OF SORROW[1]

Oswald Chambers

June 25

"What shall I say? 'Father, save Me from this hour'? But for this purpose I came to this hour. 'Father, glorify Your name' " (John 12:27–28).

As a saint of God, my attitude toward sorrow and difficulty should not be to ask that they be prevented, but to ask that God protect me so that I may remain what He created me to be, in spite of all my fires of sorrow. Our Lord received Himself, accepting His position and realizing His purpose, in the midst of the fire of sorrow. He was saved not from the hour, but out of the hour.

We say that there ought to be no sorrow, but there is sorrow, and we have to accept and receive ourselves in its fires. If we try to evade sorrow, refusing to deal with it, we are foolish. Sorrow is one of the biggest facts in life, and there is no use in saying it should not be. Sin, sorrow, and suffering are, and it is not for us to say that God has made a mistake in allowing them.

Sorrow removes a great deal of a person's shallowness, but it does not always make that person better. Suffering either gives me to myself or it destroys me. You cannot find or receive yourself through success, because you lose your head over pride. And you cannot receive yourself through the monotony of your daily life, because you give in to complaining. The only way to find yourself is in the fires of sorrow. Why it should be this way is immaterial. The fact is that it is true in the Scriptures and in human experience. You can always recognize who has been through the fires of sorrow and received himself, and you know that you can go to him in your moment of trouble and find that he has plenty of time for you. But if a person has not been through the fires of sorrow, he is apt to be contemptuous, having no respect or time for you, only turning you away.

If you will receive yourself in the fires of sorrow, God will make you nourishment for other people.

"THE SILENCE OF GOD" BY ANDREW PETERSON

(Song Summary)

When you're desperately hurting and craving God's comfort and strength, it can literally break you to hear only silence in response to your cries.

It can seem impossible to get your mind off of the things that are crushing your spirit.

Even though Jesus has told us his "yoke is easy" and his "burden is light," it often seems as though our burdens are way too heavy for us—especially when God seems absent or distant to us.

It's even harder to see other Christians apparently enjoying all the good things life has to offer—health and wealth and happiness—and have to listen to them piously tell you that Jesus has taken away all their troubles.

But you know the truth—everyone must wrestle with sorrow and trouble, and even those who follow Christ can lose their way.

It's easy to forget that Jesus experienced great troubles—think of his desperation in the Garden of Gethsemane, when he knew the horror he was about to face and yet not one of his best friends could stay awake to be with him. He's alone there, in the tyranny of the silence.

So Jesus understands—deeply—the silence and sorrow we sometimes bear alone.

God does not abandon us in that silence—soon our aching questions fade in importance, replaced by his intimate presence. Our sorrows don't have to break us—they can lead us into the very presence of God.

"JUST AS I AM" BY ANDREW PETERSON

(Song Summary)

Jesus is a heartbreaker—not, of course, in the romantic sense. But when we love him, he breaks our hearts. And he takes the broken bits and makes something beautiful grow out of them.

It's incredible that Jesus is able to take our heartbreaks and transform them into something beautiful.

Jesus has proved, over and over and over, that he knows us intimately and loves us deeply.

But we have a deep anxiety that all that is beautiful in our lives—all of the beauty Jesus is growing—can be taken away by our own terrible choices. We fear that there are limits to God's love for us, that it's ultimately a conditional love and he expects us to perform well to get it.

But then we remember the great sacrifices of Jesus, and we remember that there are no lengths he will not go to in his pursuit of us. We are loved, truly.

The "seeds" of love Jesus has planted in our lives do bear "fruit," and Jesus longs to use that fruit for the good of others in our lives. But he's not in love with our fruit—he's in love with us. He loves us, truly.

ENDNOTE 1: Taken from *My Utmost for His Highest* by Oswald Chambers, edited by James Reimann, © 1992 by Oswald Chambers Publications Assn., Ltd., and used by permission of Discovery House Publishers, Grand Rapids MI 49501. All rights reserved.

IN PURSUIT OF JESUS

WEEK 5: JESUS AND HIS FAMILY

WELCOME TO THE FAMILY

Video clip: *Cheaper By the Dozen*.

▶ Does this remind you of your family?

▶ Do you think Jesus grew up in a "normal" family?

THERE'S NO PLACE LIKE HOME

Take a moment to choose the TV or film family that best reminds you of your family of origin—the family you grew up in as a child. If you don't find one that kind of fits, think of a family from a TV show or film that does remind you of your family.

▶ *The Bradys (The Brady Bunch)*—Middle-class blended family with some sibling friction, but an underlying sense of togetherness. Strong personalities and adventurous spirits. Strong, engaged father and mother who are generally easygoing—never too intense.

▶ *The Simpsons (The Simpsons)*—Typically dysfunctional family, but not in a terribly damaging way. The problems of the parents and the kids don't obscure their ultimate underlying love and commitment to each other. One parent is a loose cannon and the other is the steadying influence in the family. Some kids are high achievers, others are not. Sometimes it seems like the family is barely holding together, yet they seem to work out their problems.

- *The Sopranos (The Sopranos)*—A highly dysfunctional family with damaging and even dangerous relationships. The family holds together, but not because of warm, intimate love for each other. Rather, fear and survival characterize the home environment. Betrayal, lying, and pragmatic brutality overshadow family closeness, though everyone seems to want it.

- *The Huxtables (The Cosby Show)*—Laughter-filled middle-class home with a strong, professional father and a nurturing, professional mother. Strong values, high expectations, and relational strength saturate the home environment. Bad decisions result in consequences that the parents won't circumvent. This home represents a "teachable moment" kind of climate. Of course, sometimes things seem almost too perfect.

- *The Waltons (The Waltons)*—A poor, hardworking, but close-knit family. Even extended family members live together. A strong work ethic and family values characterize the family, but faith in Christ seems to be more of a cultural expectation than a personal commitment. Large age span among the children, so older kids often participate in the rearing of the younger ones.

- *The von Trapps (Sound of Music)*—A family hurting from loss and sorrow, trying to cope and find their way through the darkness. The normal family system is rigid and authoritarian as a result of the wounding. One person in the family offers hope, light, and love as an alternate path.

- *The Addams (The Addams Family)*—A family full of strange and over-the-top characters who somehow all fit together. A lot of bizarre experiences characterize the growing-up years. The family "norms" seem outlandish to people outside the family, but family members have a general respect and acceptance of one another. This family has fun, but not in traditional ways.

- *The Camdens (7th Heaven)*—A strong religious household where the church and faith occupy a central place in the family's life. While the family encounters many challenges, sorrows, and joys in life, they hold together because of the parents' strength of conviction. This largely functional home still has moments of dysfunction. Parents not only tolerate doubts, struggles, and even contrary views, they explore and accept those in the family context.

Get together with a partner—someone you haven't paired up with so far in this class. Share the fictional family you chose, and tell why that TV or film family has similarities to your own.

JESUS AND HIS FAMILIES

▶ Remember our overarching pursuit—to answer Jesus' question to us: "Who do you say I am?"

You can learn a lot about people by getting to know their family.

Read the Family Matters story assigned by your leader (beginning on page 48). Read the story from your booklet, and then (if you want) reference the context of the story from the Bible later during your discussion.

With your partner, discuss the following questions:

▶ In your story, what can you learn about Jesus' relationship to family? In other words, what can you learn about the nature of his family relationships—his attitude toward family and his definition of family—from your story? Write your insights below. If your story seems thin or too easy, remember to slow down, pay attention, fuel your curiosity, and look for unexplored insights and questions. If you feel stuck, stop and simply ask God to show you the hidden treasure in the story.

▶ What's new or surprising or uncomfortable or even confusing about what your leader has written about these Family Matters stories?

▶ What can we say, broadly, about Jesus' relationship to family? How would you sum up what we've discovered?

GRAFTED INTO JESUS' FAMILY

"I am the vine; you are the branches. If a man remains in me and I in him, he will bear much fruit; apart from me you can do nothing. If anyone does not remain in me, he is like a branch that is thrown away and withers; such branches are picked up, thrown into the fire and burned. If you remain in me and my words remain in you, ask whatever you wish, and it will be given you. This is to my Father's glory, that you bear much fruit, showing yourselves to be my disciples" (John 15:5-8).

"If some of the branches have been broken off, and you, though a wild olive shoot, have been grafted in among the others and now share in the nourishing sap from the olive root, do not boast over those branches. If you do, consider this: You do not support the root, but the root supports you. You will say then, 'Branches were broken off so that I could be grafted in.' Granted. But they were broken off because of unbelief, and you stand by faith. Do not be arrogant, but be afraid. After all, if you were cut out of an olive tree that is wild by nature, and contrary to nature were grafted into a cultivated olive tree, how much more readily will these, the natural branches, be grafted into their own olive tree!" (Romans 11:17-20, 24).

THE PROCESS OF GRAFTING

This is how the professionals who work for nurseries describe the process and requirements for grafting….

- ▶ First you need a hardy "root stock." This plant is vigorous and full of life energy.
- ▶ When you graft, you typically choose a weaker or less hardy plant to graft into the stronger and acclimated root.
- ▶ Professionals typically use grafting only when they want to make a hybrid plant: "a new creature." For example, they might create a unique plant that can live and thrive in a particular climate with stronger roots than the original plant's natural ones.
- ▶ Grafting is an art. It's not easy to make a graft work. You need to know what you're doing and exercise a lot of patience. If you approach the process quickly or haphazardly, the graft won't take.

▶ When you graft, you cut a branch from the weaker plant or tree. Then you join that open cut to an open cut on the stronger or root tree. This is an intimate process. It reminds us of what Jesus said: "I am the bridegroom, you are my bride." "I am the vine, you are [my grafted] branches."

▶ Finally, over time, the life of the grafted branch becomes part of the life of the strong plant or tree. Often, the weaker graft actually falls away after a successful graft. Its life is transferred to the root—hidden in it and part of a new species.

A MEDITATION ON GRAFTING

Quietly consider the questions your leader asks while you explore the cutting you're holding. Close your eyes, and just open them to look closely at your cutting or to make notes below.

▶ What do you feel? Does it feel tender, vulnerable, exposed, or raw? What other words would you use to describe the cut?

▶ Do you sense evidence of "the root's" new life flowing into you? Ask God for the evidence. Write it here.

CLOSING WORSHIP

Chris Tomlin's "Mighty Is the Power of the Cross." If you'd like to follow along with a song summary, turn to page 50.

FAMILY MATTERS

▶ **Jesus' Genealogy** (Matthew 1:1-17)—The Bible lists 42 generations from Abraham to David to Joseph to Jesus—42 generations! In your Bible, look at the list of names listed in Jesus' genealogy. What names do you recognize, and what do you know about those people?

▶ **Jesus Stays Behind at the Temple** (Luke 2:41-52)—"Every year [Jesus'] parents went to Jerusalem for the Feast of the Passover. When he was twelve years old, they went up to the Feast, according to the custom. After the Feast was over, while his parents were returning home, the boy Jesus stayed behind in Jerusalem, but they were unaware of it. Thinking he was in their company, they traveled on for a day. Then they began looking for him among their relatives and friends. When they did not find him, they went back to Jerusalem to look for him. After three days they found him in the temple courts, sitting among the teachers, listening to them and asking them questions. Everyone who heard him was amazed at his understanding and his answers. When his parents saw him, they were astonished. His mother said to him, 'Son, why have you treated us like this? Your father and I have been anxiously searching for you.' 'Why were you searching for me?' he asked. 'Didn't you know I had to be in my Father's house?' But they did not understand what he was saying to them. Then he went down to Nazareth with them and was obedient to them. But his mother treasured all these things in her heart. And Jesus grew in wisdom and stature, and in favor with God and men."

▶ **Jesus Turns Water Into Wine for His Mother** (John 2:1-5)—"On the third day a wedding took place at Cana in Galilee. Jesus' mother was there, and Jesus and his disciples had also been invited to the wedding. When the wine was gone, Jesus' mother said to him, 'They have no more wine.' 'Dear woman, why do you involve me?' Jesus replied. 'My time has not yet come.' His mother said to the servants, 'Do whatever he tells you.' "

▶ **The Cost of Following Jesus Includes Family Obligations** (Matthew 8:18-22)—"When Jesus saw the crowd around him, he gave orders to cross to the other side of the lake. Then a teacher of the law came to him and said, 'Teacher, I will follow you wherever you go.' Jesus replied, 'Foxes have holes and birds of the air have nests, but the Son of Man has no place to lay his head.' Another disciple said to him, 'Lord, first let me go and bury my father.' But Jesus told him, 'Follow me, and let the dead bury their own dead.' "

▶ **Jesus Comes With a Sword, Not Peace** (Matthew 10:34-39)—"Do not suppose that I have come to bring peace to the earth. I did not come to bring peace, but a sword. For I have come to turn 'a man against his father, a daughter against her mother, a daughter-in-law against her mother-in-law—a man's enemies will be the members of his own household.' Anyone who loves his father or mother more than me is not worthy of me; anyone who loves his son or daughter more than me is not worthy of me; and anyone who does not take his cross and follow me is not worthy of me. Whoever finds his life will lose it, and whoever loses his life for my sake will find it."

▶ **Who Are My True Mother and Brothers?** (Matthew 12:46-50)—"While Jesus was still talking to the crowd, his mother and brothers stood outside, wanting to speak to him. Someone told him, 'Your mother and brothers are standing outside, wanting to speak to you.' He replied to him, 'Who is my mother, and who are my brothers?' Pointing to his disciples, he said, 'Here are my mother and my brothers. For whoever does the will of my Father in heaven is my brother and sister and mother.' "

▶ **Jesus Creates a New Family** (John 19:25-27)—"Near the cross of Jesus stood his mother, his mother's sister, Mary the wife of Clopas, and Mary Magdalene. When Jesus saw his mother there, and the disciple whom he loved standing nearby, he said to his mother, 'Dear woman, here is your son,' and to the disciple, 'Here is your mother.' From that time on, this disciple took her into his home."

"MIGHTY IS THE POWER OF THE CROSS"
BY CHRIS TOMLIN

(Song Summary)

We look for life in so many places—we're desperate for things that will make us feel alive, heal our wounds, take away our blame, fill up our emptiness, and make us whole. But what is powerful enough to do all that?

Well, Jesus' sacrifice—his willing slaughter—on the cross is the only thing powerful enough to do all that.

But, again, we wonder what can rebuild our faith, or show us God's love, or bring us back when we stray, or make our hardened hearts soft again, or release us from the penalty of our own destructive actions? What, really, can save us?

Well, Jesus' sacrifice—his willing slaughter—on the cross is the only thing powerful enough to do all that.

I don't claim to understand this—I just know it's true.

Jesus—only Jesus—is powerful enough to redeem us, and he did it by laying down his power and strength to willingly sacrifice himself on our behalf.

Jesus is our rescuer, our deliverer, our healer, our great Love.

IN PURSUIT OF JESUS

WEEK 6: JESUS AND SATAN'S FAMILY

DIFFERENT MISSIONS

"The thief comes only to steal and kill and destroy; I have come that they may have life, and have it to the full" (John 10:10).

"Have you ever wondered why Jesus married those two statements? Did you even know he spoke them at the same time? I mean, he says them in one breath. And he has his reasons. By all means, God intends life for you. But right now that life is *opposed*. It doesn't just roll in on a tray. There is a thief. He comes to steal and kill and destroy. In other words, yes, the offer is life, but you're going to have to fight for it because there's an Enemy in your life with a different agenda. There *is* something set against us." [1]

—JOHN ELDREDGE

WHAT DO WE KNOW ABOUT SATAN?

▶ What do these familiar names for Satan really mean?

▶ How did Satan become God's enemy?

WHAT FORCES SHAPED SATAN?

"And there was war in heaven. Michael and his angels fought against the dragon, and the dragon and his angels fought back. But he was not strong enough, and they lost their place in heaven. The great dragon was hurled down—that ancient serpent called the devil, or Satan, who leads the whole world astray. He was hurled to the earth, and his angels with him" (Revelation 12:7-9).

▶ Satan loved his own beauty more than God.

▶ Defeated, Satan can no longer directly assault God. Because he wants to still hurt God, Satan turns his attention to God's children.

"When the dragon saw that he had been hurled to the earth, he pursued the woman who had given birth to the male child" (Revelation 12:13).

THE FATHER OF LIES (FILM CLIPS)

▶ What parallels do you see between Salieri and Satan?

▶ What lies does Scar tell Simba?

▶ How do these reflect the lies Satan tells us?

▶ If nothing changes in Simba's story, how will this lie eventually affect him?

▶ What's the impact of Satan's lies in our lives?

JESUS INTERACTING WITH SATAN

"The reason the Son of God appeared was to destroy the devil's work" (1 John 3:8b).

"Next Jesus was taken into the wild by the Spirit for the Test. The Devil was ready to give it. Jesus prepared for the Test by fasting forty days and forty nights. That left him, of course, in a state of extreme hunger, which the Devil took advantage of in the first test: 'Since you are God's Son, speak the word that will turn these stones into loaves of bread.'

"Jesus answered by quoting Deuteronomy: 'It takes more than bread to stay alive. It takes a steady stream of words from God's mouth.'

"For the second test the Devil took him to the Holy City. He sat him on top of the Temple and said, 'Since you are God's Son, jump.' The Devil goaded him by quoting Psalm 91: 'He has placed you in the care of angels. They will catch you so that you won't so much as stub your toe on a stone.'

"Jesus countered with another citation from Deuteronomy: 'Don't you dare test the Lord your God.'

"For the third test, the Devil took him to the peak of a huge mountain. He gestured expansively, pointing out all the earth's kingdoms, how glorious they all were. Then he said, 'They're yours—lock, stock, and barrel. Just go down on your knees and worship me, and they're yours.'

"Jesus' refusal was curt: 'Beat it, Satan!' He backed his rebuke with a third quotation from Deuteronomy: 'Worship the Lord your God, and only him. Serve him with absolute single-heartedness.'

"The Test was over. The Devil left. And in his place, angels! Angels came and took care of Jesus' needs" (Matthew 4:1-11, *The Message*).

▶ What different ways did Satan try to attack and destroy Jesus in the wilderness?

▶ Why would Satan attack Jesus in these ways?

- ▶ What assumptions does Satan make about why Jesus has come?

- ▶ What assumptions does Satan make about Jesus' heart?

- ▶ Why did Jesus respond to Satan the way he did?

- ▶ Why did Jesus use Scripture to respond to Satan?

- ▶ Unlike his interactions with the Pharisees, Jesus never raised his voice or got angry or called Satan names. Why?

JESUS CASTING OUT DEMONS

If your leader decides your class has time, refer to "Jesus Destroying the Works of Satan" on page 55. Then consider the following questions:

- ▶ What can we learn about responding to Satan's influence in our lives from the way Jesus responded to Satan and his "family"?

- ▶ What does Jesus want to communicate about himself with his actions?

THE TRUTH SETS YOU FREE (FILM CLIP)

As you watch what Simba learns from Rafiki and Mufasa, reflect on the important role remembering Jesus plays in our lives.

JESUS DESTROYING THE WORKS OF SATAN

▶ Jesus is mocked and "outed" by a demon, but he muzzles the demon (Luke 4:33-35).

▶ Jesus casts demons out of "many" early in ministry (Luke 4:41).

▶ Jesus casts a "mob" of demons out of Gerasene man (Luke 8:26-36).

▶ Jesus casts out a demon from a possessed boy (Luke 9:38-43).

▶ Jesus' disciples say, "Even the demons are subject to us!" (Luke 10:17-20, NAS).

▶ Jesus tells Peter, "Get behind me, Satan!...You are not setting your mind on God's interests, but man's" (Matthew 16:23, NAS).

▶ The Pharisees accuse Jesus of using Satan's power to exorcise (Luke 11:14-26).

▶ Jesus casts out a demon from a woman on the Sabbath (Luke 13:10-16).

▶ Jesus allows Satan to "sift" Peter (Luke 22:31-34). Satan demands permission, and God gives Satan room to move against Peter, but only for God's greater purposes in Peter's life. Satan is constrained, just as he was constrained in his attacks on Job.

ENDNOTE 1: John Eldredge, *Waking the Dead: The Glory of a Heart Fully Alive* (Thomas Nelson, 2003), p. 13.

IN PURSUIT OF JESUS

WEEK 7: JESUS AND HIS TRUE MISSION

WELCOME

Listen to "Why It Matters" by Sara Groves. You can follow along with the song summary on page 59.

▶ What do the words "protest of the darkness" mean in this song? How might Jesus be a "protest of the darkness"?

▶ What do we really know about Jesus' true mission on earth?

EXPLORE JESUS THROUGH STORY

We're most familiar with pursuing Jesus through propositional truths. *Proposition* means, literally, a "statement that affirms or denies something." So a propositional truth is simply a statement about truth. Essentially, we tear apart the larger story of the gospel so we can break it into lists and statements of what we should and shouldn't do as Christians.

Approaching the story of Jesus propositionally does reveal truths—with a small t. But this propositional approach does not, by itself, get at the Truth with a capital T. The Bible isn't written *primarily* propositionally. Rather, Scripture is written as a collection of stories that ultimately point to Jesus.

DONALD MILLER

"I wrapped this book [*Searching for God Knows What*] up [on a] night I felt like I was losing it a bit. Essentially, I had begun to wonder if I had misunderstood the gospel of Jesus, thinking of it in propositional terms rather than relational dynamics. The latter seemed too poetic to be true, but the former had been killing my soul for years and was simply illogical. If we hold that Jesus wanted us to 'believe' certain ideas or 'do' certain things in order to be a Christian, we are holding to heresy…I finished the last paragraph and felt a kind of sickness at the thought of whether or not I was telling the truth. But after further consideration, and after rewriting the book, I realized the formulaic version of Christianity was irrational, and for that matter, unbiblical. True Christian spirituality mirrors relational dynamics more than the workings of a free-market economy. This seemed to open up an entire new world to me, a world where every thought and feeling operates as a kind of living metaphor for the workings of the Godhead.

"As a year has passed since the release of the book, I've seen more and more how, in my own life and in the lives of the Christians around me, we subscribe to false gospels that are troubling our souls. Because we live in a constant sales environment where we are told a certain car will make us sexy or a certain dishwashing detergent will be a miracle for our dishes, we assume the gospel of Jesus works the same way, that is, if we invest something, we get something more back. But this is not the case. To understand what the Bible explains Jesus' gospel to be, we must look to each other, to the way a father interacts with a child, a bride to a bridegroom, a doctor to a patient. When we let go of the idea of Jesus as a product and embrace Him as a being, our path to spiritual maturity begins." [1]

CLUES TO JESUS' TRUE MISSION (FILM CLIP)

The 1998 film version of *Les Misérables* follows the story of ex-convict Jean Valjean, a man imprisoned in France to 19 years of hard labor for stealing a loaf of bread for his hungry family. Valjean gains his release from prison, but he can't get a job because he's an ex-convict. He resorts to stealing from a kind bishop who invites him into his home. Valjean injures the bishop when he's caught stealing. In a powerful scene, the bishop keeps Valjean from going to jail—literally, the bishop redeems Valjean and challenges him to live his life for God.

From that point on, Valjean lives passionately for God and for the poor and oppressed. He becomes a successful businessman and political leader. When, without Valjean's knowledge, one of his factory workers is wrongfully fired from her job at his factory, she descends into poverty and prostitution and bitterness toward Valjean, because she believes he ordered her firing. In this long scene you'll see Fantine, the young woman, struggle to stay alive on the street just before she meets Valjean again.

▶ What makes it difficult for Fantine to trust that Valjean wants to offer her a pure love?

▶ What must happen in Fantine, the prostitute, to allow Valjean to love her?

▶ What obstacles must Valjean overcome to convince Fantine to receive real love from him?

▶ What does Valjean do to convince Fantine to be loved by him? to woo her?

▶ If we treat Valjean as a symbol for Christ and Fantine as a symbol for us, what can we learn about Jesus' true mission on earth from this story?

JESUS' HIGH PRIESTLY PRAYER

Follow along as your leader reads this prayer on page 60. Or if your group runs out of time, read the prayer on your own during the upcoming week.

CLOSING

Listen to the Michael Card song "Jesus Let Us Come to Know You."

"WHY IT MATTERS" BY SARA GROVES

(Song Summary)

I need to hear the story of God's redemptive love again—it's so easy for me to forget it all. Not because I literally forget it, but because I know it so well that I take it for granted. I forget how beautiful, and how powerful, God's story really is.

Remind me again of why our paltry little efforts to reflect the goodness of that story still matter so much—remind me again of how important it is to tell others of the beauty of God's story.

In the midst of terror and hardship and tragedy, we must remind ourselves of the greater truth—of the real and present beauty of God's love for us. When we do, it's our way of protesting the lies and destruction of God's enemy.

It's the little acts of love and beauty that really matter—that remind us of God's greater acts of love and beauty. We need these tiny acts of beauty like we need little footholds on a sheer cliff. Sometimes all we need is a tiny, solid foothold to keep us from falling.

ENDNOTE 1: From Donald Miller's explanation of why he wrote *Searching for God Knows What*, on his Web site www.donaldmillerwords.com.

JESUS' HIGH PRIESTLY PRAYER

John 17:1-12, 20-26 (The Message)

Jesus said these things. Then, raising his eyes in prayer, he said:

Father, it's time.

Display the bright splendor of your Son

So the Son in turn may show your bright splendor.

You put him in charge of everything human

So he might give real and eternal life to all in his charge.

And this is the real and eternal life:

That they know you,

The one and only true God,

And Jesus Christ, whom you sent.

I glorified you on earth

By completing down to the last detail

What you assigned me to do.

And now, Father, glorify me with your very own splendor,

The very splendor I had in your presence

Before there was a world.

I spelled out your character in detail

To the men and women you gave me.

They were yours in the first place;

Then you gave them to me,

And they have now done what you said.

They know now, beyond the shadow of a doubt,

That everything you gave me is firsthand from you,

For the message you gave me, I gave them;

And they took it, and were convinced

That I came from you.

They believed that you sent me.

I pray for them.
I'm not praying for the God-rejecting world
But for those you gave me,
For they are yours by right.
Everything mine is yours, and yours mine,
And my life is on display in them.
For I'm no longer going to be visible in the world;
They'll continue in the world
While I return to you.
Holy Father, guard them as they pursue this life
That you conferred as a gift through me,
So they can be one heart and mind
As we are one heart and mind.
As long as I was with them, I guarded them
In the pursuit of the life you gave through me;
I even posted a night watch.
And not one of them got away,
Except for the rebel bent on destruction
(the exception that proved the rule of Scripture).
I'm praying not only for them
But also for those who will believe in me
Because of them and their witness about me.
The goal is for all of them to become one heart and mind—
Just as you, Father, are in me and I in you,
So they might be one heart and mind with us.
Then the world might believe that you, in fact, sent me.
The same glory you gave me, I gave them,
So they'll be as unified and together as we are—
I in them and you in me.
Then they'll be mature in this oneness,

And give the godless world evidence
That you've sent me and loved them
In the same way you've loved me.
Father, I want those you gave me
To be with me, right where I am,
So they can see my glory, the splendor you gave me,
Having loved me
Long before there ever was a world.
Righteous Father, the world has never known you,
But I have known you, and these disciples know
That you sent me on this mission.
I have made your very being known to them—
Who you are and what you do—
And continue to make it known,
So that your love for me
Might be in them
Exactly as I am in them.

WEEK 8: JESUS ACTING SUPERNATURALLY

WELCOME

Find a partner roughly your own size, and participate in the activity as your leader instructs.

▶ How is what happened to you like or unlike a supernatural experience?

SPIDEY GETS STRETCHED

Watch the scene from *Spiderman 2*. Spiderman's archenemy, Doc Ock, has sabotaged a hurtling train. All of the passengers on the train will die unless Spiderman can save them.

▶ What emotions did you feel toward Spiderman as you watched this clip? List below all the emotions you felt as you watched.

▶ Why do you think we're oblivious to Spiderman's ability to intentionally harm the people on the train?

DO WE REALLY BELIEVE?

Follow along as your leader reads this story by Mark Galli from his book *Jesus Mean and Wild:* [1]

"After we read the passage in which Jesus calms the storm, I began as I usually did with more theologically sophisticated groups: I asked them about the storms in their lives. There was a puzzled look among my Laotian friends, so I elaborated: we all have storms—problems, worries, troubles, crises—and this story teaches that Jesus can give us peace in the midst of those storms. 'So what are your storms?' I asked.

"Again, more puzzled silence. Finally, one of the men hesitantly asked, 'Do you mean that Jesus actually calmed the wind and sea in the middle of a storm?'

"I thought he was finding the story incredulous, and I didn't want to get distracted with the problem of miracles. So I replied, 'Yes, but we should not get hung up on the details of the miracle. We should remember that Jesus can calm the storms in our lives.'

"Another stretch of awkward silence ensued until another replied, 'Well, if Jesus calmed the wind and the waves, he must be a very powerful man!' At this, they all nodded vigorously and chattered excitedly to one another in Lao. Except for me, the room was full of awe and wonder.

"I suddenly realized that they grasped the story better than I did, and I finally acknowledged, 'Yes, Jesus is a very powerful person. In fact, Christians believe he is the Creator of heaven and earth, and thus, of course, he has power over the wind and the waves.' "

▶ If we're honest, we're a lot like Mark Galli. Why do we so often struggle to believe in the literal power of Jesus in our lives?

THE SUPERNATURAL ACTS OF JESUS

- ▶ Jesus changes water into wine at the Cana wedding (John 2:1-11).
- ▶ Jesus commands a miraculous catch of fish for the first disciples (Luke 5:4-9).
- ▶ Jesus calls Nathanael by telling him he "saw" Nathanael when he was too far away to see (John 1:43-49).
- ▶ Jesus seems to know the thoughts of others (Matthew 9:1-4).
- ▶ Jesus feeds the 5,000 with a few loaves and fish (Matthew 14:15-21).
- ▶ Jesus walks on the sea in full view of his disciples (Matthew 14:22-33).
- ▶ Jesus feeds the 4,000 with a few loaves and fish (Matthew 15:32-38).
- ▶ Jesus curses the fig tree, and it withers on the spot (Matthew 21:18-20).

Find two other people and form a trio. Then discuss your assigned question from one of the following:[2]

(Remember the habits of our pursuit—our tasting skills. Slow down, fuel your curiosity, pay attention to details, ask more questions. As a trio, come up with a detailed answer to the question your leader assigns.)

- ▶ If Jesus could walk on water, why didn't he ever fly? (John 6:15-21)
- ▶ Jesus' first recorded miracle was turning the water into wine at a wedding feast in Cana. This almost seems like a party trick rather than an appropriate use of his authority and ability, so why did he do it? (John 2:1-11)
- ▶ Twice Jesus fed a huge crowd with just a few loaves and some fish. Why didn't Jesus produce food in this way for every meal he ate? (Matthew 14:13-21)
- ▶ If Jesus had played sports, would he have been good enough to compete in the Olympics? Why or why not? (John 6:19)
- ▶ Do you think Jesus really knew the hidden thoughts of people, or did he have no more knowledge of others than we do? Explain. (Matthew 9:1-4)
- ▶ Did Jesus need to learn how to read or how to do math, or did he just know these things intrinsically? Explain. (John 16:30)
- ▶ At one point, Jesus tells Nathanael that he could see Nathanael sitting under a fig tree before he'd ever met him—a supernatural feat. Did Jesus have "superpowers"

like a comic book hero? If so, what were they? If not, how do you explain his ability to see someone too far away to see? (John 1:43-51)

ANNIE DILLARD

"On the whole, I do not find Christians, outside of the catacombs, sufficiently sensible of the conditions. Does anyone have the foggiest idea of what sort of power we so blithely invoke? Or, as I suspect, does no one believe a word of it?" [3]

▶ When the paralytic in John 5:1-9—who had camped out by the pool of Bethsaida for many years hoping to be healed—asked Jesus to heal him, why did Jesus *first* ask him if he really wanted to be healed?

MARK GALLI

"This simplistic answer [of Mark Galli to the Laotians' question about Jesus' power] would not have gone over in some of the more sophisticated congregations of which I've been a part. As I noted, it didn't go over with me until I was confronted with my unbelief. The reasons for that are complex, but I think one is that the power of Christ frightens us—as well it should. And we'll do anything to avoid facing it as an ongoing reality, much to our loss." [4]

CLOSING MEDITATION

Close your eyes, and ask God the following question. Journal what you "hear."

▶ God, am I frightened by your power? If so, why? If not, why not?

Listen to the song "Serve Hymn/Holy Is the Lord" from Andrew Peterson's album *Love and Thunder* as a worship response to Jesus. If you'd like to follow along with the song summary, see below.

"SERVE HYMN/HOLY IS THE LORD" BY ANDREW PETERSON

(Song Summary)

My sins, I know, are so obvious and destructive and big that it's overwhelming to think of them.

I've hurt the One who loves me best so deeply—I'm not sure anything can make it right.

But God's love is so powerful, so deep, so all-encompassing that it can overshadow—more like swallow—the destructive consequences of my sin.

His great love for me makes me want to serve him all the days of my life—his fierce rescue of me has given me a treasured hope.

Now I'm learning to appreciate—even treasure—every moment, every breath I take, and every created beauty around me. And that's all because I've tasted his over-shadowing love and grace in my life.

God is so glorious, but in his humility he didn't let his glory be a barrier between us. In his mercy he stooped low to scoop me up.

Jesus...well, I just don't deserve the love of such a glorious King. It makes me want to serve him all the days of my life. It makes me want to gush with praise about him. Only Jesus is good, through and through.

ENDNOTE 1: Mark Galli, *Jesus Mean and Wild: The Unexpected Love of an Untamable God* (Baker Books, 2006), p. 112.
ENDNOTE 2: These questions are taken from *JCQs:150 Jesus-Centered Questions* by Rick Lawrence (Group Publishing, 2006).
ENDNOTE 3: Annie Dillard, *Teaching a Stone to Talk* (Harper & Row, 1982), p. 52.
ENDNOTE 4: Mark Galli, *Jesus Mean and Wild: The Unexpected Love of an Untamable God* (Baker Books, 2006), p. 112.

IN PURSUIT OF JESUS

WEEK 9: JESUS, THE SLAUGHTERED LAMB

THE NAMES OF JESUS

▶ What names of Jesus can you remember?

JESUS "THE LAMB OF GOD"

▶ Isaiah 53:7-8: "He was oppressed and afflicted, yet he did not open his mouth; he was led like a lamb to the slaughter, and as a sheep before her shearers is silent, so he did not open his mouth. By oppression and judgment he was taken away. And who can speak of his descendants? For he was cut off from the land of the living; for the transgression of my people he was stricken."

▶ John 1:29: "The next day John [the Baptist] saw Jesus coming toward him and said, 'Look, the Lamb of God, who takes away the sin of the world!' "

▶ 1 Peter 1:18-19: "For you know that it was not with perishable things such as silver or gold that you were redeemed from the empty way of life handed down to you from your forefathers, but with the precious blood of Christ, a lamb without blemish or defect."

▶ Revelation 5–7 (excerpts): In the vision John records in the book of Revelation, he hears a mighty angel ask, "Who is worthy to break the seals and open the scroll?" (5:2). He goes on to observe: "Then I saw a Lamb, looking as if it had been slain, standing in the center of the throne, encircled by the four living creatures and the elders" (5:6). And then ends this portion of his vision with:

"For the Lamb at the center of the throne will be their shepherd; he will lead them to springs of living water. And God will wipe away every tear from their eyes" (7:17).

THREE VIEWS OF THE SLAUGHTERED LAMB

1. Study, for five minutes, the copy of the painting *Agnus Dei* by the artist Francisco Zurbarán.

   ▶ What do you notice?

   ▶ What do you see that supports your perceptions, knowledge, and experience of Jesus?

   ▶ What do you see that does not support your perceptions, knowledge, and experience of Jesus?

2. Study the "death" of Obi-Wan Kenobi in *Star Wars*.

   ▶ What do you notice in this scene that sheds light on Jesus as the "Lamb of God"?

   ▶ What in this scene supports your perceptions, knowledge, and experience of Jesus?

   ▶ What in this scene does not support your perceptions, knowledge, and experience of Jesus?

3. Study the parables around you. Go anywhere you want for the next seven minutes. Wander until something captures your eye or ear. As soon as you notice
   something, stop and simply ask God to show you if he's providing a parable
   offering insight into Jesus as the slaughtered Lamb. You might find something
   or not—don't worry about it. This isn't a test. We're just playing.

   ▶ What did you notice, and how might it be a parable for the slaughtered Lamb?

THE UPWARD/DOWNWARD PATH TO SLAUGHTER

Jesus gave up his life of his own will; no one took it from him.

Going Up: Jesus reveals himself, but consciously does things to delay his arrest and
execution. In John 8:20-21, Jesus reveals his true identity. But the authorities don't seize
him "because his time had not yet come." This happens many times on his upward journey to a turning point in his public ministry. (See John 7:1-30 and John 10:39.)

John 8:20-21: " 'You do not know me or my Father,' Jesus replied. 'If you knew me,
you would know my Father also.' He spoke these words while teaching in the temple
area near the place where the offerings were put. Yet no one seized him, because his time
had not yet come. Once more Jesus said to them, 'I am going away, and you will look for
me, and you will die in your sin. Where I go, you cannot come.' "

The Turning Point: Jesus determines when the time is right to move toward death. In
Matthew 12:9-15a, Jesus heals a man with a withered hand on the Sabbath. He appears
to do this to purposely antagonize the powerful Jewish leaders of Jerusalem. Only when
Jesus enters Jerusalem—the seat of political power—does he become a real threat. This
is the start of his downward journey to the cross.

Matthew 12:9-15a: "Going on from that place, he went into their synagogue, and a
man with a shriveled hand was there. Looking for a reason to accuse Jesus, they asked
him, 'Is it lawful to heal on the Sabbath?' He said to them, 'If any of you has a sheep and
it falls into a pit on the Sabbath, will you not take hold of it and lift it out? How much
more valuable is a man than a sheep! Therefore it is lawful to do good on the Sabbath.'

Then he said to the man, 'Stretch out your hand.' So he stretched it out and it was completely restored, just as sound as the other. But the Pharisees went out and plotted how they might kill Jesus. Aware of this, Jesus withdrew from that place."

Going Down: Now Jesus intentionally does things to get himself killed. In John 11:47-50, the high priest Caiaphas hatches the death plot against Jesus, saying, "It is expedient for you that one man die for the people" (NAS). Later, in John 18:19-24, Jesus seals his own death by purposely provoking the high priest. He answers the high priest's questions with what the guards take as insolence, so one of them slaps him. Finally, in Matthew 27:11-26, Pilate tries hard to release Jesus. But Jesus outsmarts him and ensures his own execution.

John 18:19-24: "Meanwhile, the high priest questioned Jesus about his disciples and his teaching. 'I have spoken openly to the world,' Jesus replied. 'I always taught in synagogues or at the temple, where all the Jews come together. I said nothing in secret. Why question me? Ask those who heard me. Surely they know what I said.' When Jesus said this, one of the officials nearby struck him in the face. 'Is this the way you answer the high priest?' he demanded. 'If I said something wrong,' Jesus replied, 'testify as to what is wrong. But if I spoke the truth, why did you strike me?' Then Annas sent him, still bound, to Caiaphas the high priest."

CLOSING WORSHIP

Listen to "Behold the Lamb of God" by Andrew Peterson. If you'd like to follow along with the song summary, turn to page 72.

"BEHOLD THE LAMB OF GOD"
BY ANDREW PETERSON

(Song Summary)

Stare long and hard at Jesus, who gave himself up to be slaughtered on the cross—of his own free will.

His sacrifice gives us hope and life and lights our darkness. His sacrifice has taken away the penalty of death for our sins.

In our wayward acts of betrayal, we've strayed so far and damaged our own hearts so deeply. We so desperately need a rescuer.

And Jesus is that rescuer! He's our only hope. We're entirely dependent on his goodness toward us. We could never ask him to do what he did willingly—to give up all he had and endure the torture of the cross on our behalf.

There is no one like Jesus!

IN PURSUIT OF JESUS

WEEK 10: JESUS, POST-RESURRECTION

OUR BIG PURSUIT

Who do I say Jesus is?

Listen to "God's Own Fool" by Michael Card. Turn to the song summary on page 76.

We almost always think of foolishness as a bad thing. How and why did Michael Card use it as a positive description of Jesus in this song?

FILM CLIP

Watch the scene from Charles Dickens' *A Christmas Carol,* when Ebenezer Scrooge received a visit from the ghost of his old partner, Jacob Marley. Then answer:

▶ How plausible, or not, is Dickens' picture of the afterlife?

THE THREE QUESTIONS

Read Luke 24 and John 20–21, and on your own, answer the following questions:

▶ Group 1: What did Jesus *really* say? What if Jesus said these things with a totally different inflection or tone than you've always assumed?

▶ Group 2: What did Jesus *really* do? What if Jesus did these things for totally different reasons than you've always assumed?

▶ Group 3: How did others *really* react to Jesus? What if *you* were one of the people experiencing Jesus in these passages?

GROUP DISCUSSIONS

Gather with the others in the class who were assigned the same number. Together, pursue insights, truths, common threads, surprises, and profound ah-ha moments as your group answers the questions:

▶ Group 1: Why did Jesus say these things?

▶ Group 2: Why did Jesus do these things?

▶ Group 3: Why did others react to Jesus the ways they did?

Interact with the answers of the other groups. You might ask and answer some of the following questions to help you along:

▶ What's something you like about a group's answer?

▶ What's something you don't like, or disagree with?

▶ What's missing from their answer?

▶ From what the group shared, what really sticks out to you about Jesus?

▶ If we had only this information about Jesus, how would we answer his question "Who do you say I am?"

ANSWERING THE BIG QUESTION

Who do we say Jesus is?

CLOSING

After your class prays, listen to "Joy in the Journey" by Michael Card. You'll find a song summary on page 77 if you want to reflect on the meaning of the words later, after the class has ended.

"GOD'S OWN FOOL"
BY MICHAEL CARD

(Song Summary)

I've always thought of Jesus as the wisest man who ever lived, but God himself has described wisdom as seeming "foolish" to most people—that means Jesus was the biggest fool of all!

Pretty much everyone in Jesus' life thought, at one time or another, he was crazy. He said and did things that made absolutely no sense to people.

We're all like little children who think we know it all already—but Jesus cured our blindness by "playing the fool." For example, he showed his strength by choosing weakness. His example draws us to him—makes us want to follow him. Something in us is "foolish" as well—we recognize God's foolishness is really the deepest wisdom, and we want to live as he lives.

To gain everything—to live as a fool for God—we must die to our own wisdom, our own self-sufficiency, and give everything over to Jesus. When we do, we'll find ourselves living in a faith adventure, and we'll know what it is to suffer on his behalf.

If we give up our "right" to understand everything—if, instead, we act on our passionate attraction to Jesus and commit ourselves to believing in his "foolish wisdom," our eyes will be opened to his truth.

We can't help but follow Jesus, because he's planted in our hearts a love for his truth, his goodness, his wisdom.

"JOY IN THE JOURNEY" BY MICHAEL CARD

(Song Summary)

Life isn't just about the "end"—there's so much joy locked up in our along-the-way experiences. For example, God's truths are like a light in the darkness. And our lives are full of mystery and adventure. And when we do what God asks us to do, we experience a deep sense of freedom.

If you're looking for forgiveness, you'll find it when you believe in the Forgiver. And if you're looking for a light at the end of your personal tunnel, you'll find it in the Father of Lights.

So for everyone who's committed him- or herself to God—who now shares his eternal life even while you're stuck dealing with the impact of sin in your life—don't forget God's promise to you, that you'll live with him as his own son or daughter forevermore. Of course, a life committed to following Jesus won't be easy, but don't forget how far you had wandered from his love.

It's worth repeating...Life isn't just about the "end"—there's so much joy locked up in our along-the-way experiences. For example, God's truths are like a light in the darkness. And our lives are full of mystery and adventure. And when we do what God asks us to do, we experience a deep sense of freedom.

NOTES:

NOTES:

NOTES: